Common Sense Gun Control

The middle ground for effective gun control proposed by a Professional Engineer and licensed gunsmith.

By
Ralph L. Stephenson, BS, MS, PE

Version 3.0, Completely revised and updated from previous editions

Forward

Recent mass killings by terrorists and mentally ill people using guns and the increasing murder rate, particularly of school children and policemen, and in a few cases by policemen, has increased the public awareness of the need for more gun controls. Many politicians are now openly calling for such.

There is no doubt that there is a need to keep terrorists, mentally unstable persons, and known criminals from possessing guns. How to do it is the issue.

This book will probably anger both those who are against any form of gun control and those who wish all guns made illegal to own. This book presents a middle ground, a common sense approach to control guns. Methods to keep guns out of the hands of mentally ill, terrorists, criminals, and young people who for reasons that cannot be fathomed, kill large numbers of innocent children and adults will be recommended.

Of course, acts of violence using guns cannot be prevented completely, however, it can be made much more difficult for violent people to obtain guns while preserving the rights of responsible citizens to own guns.

Full disclosure, I have owned and used guns all my life. I still own a few guns. I used to hunt, am still a licensed Gunsmith, and am a former member of the National Rifle Association. I am a former member of the Texas State Rifle Association as well. I hold a Federal Firearms License and am also a licensed Professional Engineer. I have never, however, approved of, nor taken part in, nor funded any of the activities of the NRA's political action wing, which I consider to hold extreme positions. I remained a member of the NRA because membership included insurance and a subscription to a technical magazine. I recommend all gun owners obtain insurance. I ignored the ridiculous extremist ranting's on the editorial pages of the NRA magazines.

I used to have an extensive gun collection intended to show the evolution of guns from flintlocks to modern weapons. I am mobility impaired and am no longer able to hunt and no longer had need of so many guns so I sold them at auction through a licensed dealer. I kept a few for home protection. I used to make guns, mostly black powder guns, for sport, and have modified many guns for various purposes, mostly to make military rifles into sporting rifles, add accessories such as scopes and stocks to guns, and other gunsmith work.

I come from a very long line of German Blacksmiths and Gunsmiths. My ancestors fought in the Revolutionary War and serviced guns for Washington's army. My ancestors also served in Grant's Army during the Civil War as blacksmiths. Half of the men who volunteered for service from my family was killed in action in World War Two, and one fourth were wounded. All males of service age in my family served voluntarily. We understand both guns and the price of freedom. But freedom is not free and certainly not without the obligation of individuals to behave responsibility.

Some of the gun laws are, quite frankly, ridiculous, and should be repealed, however, many laws should be kept. There is a movement under way to repeal many of these laws. While I agree that some need changing, mass repeals will only exacerbate the present situation, which is getting and will continue to get worse.

Initially, I wasn't going to write this book, however, my life is near its end. If this book helps prevent one mass shooting it will be worth the hassle it will likely cause me.

Please read this book with an open mind and I believe you will see the logic and common sense it represents.

8

The Author

Table of Contents

Chapter 1 – Gun Control Laws, History, and Common Sense

The following is the briefest of overviews of a very large subject.

The Second Amendment of 1791

The basis for the legality of guns in the Unites States is the Second Amendment to the Constitution, which was ratified in 1791, and reads:

"A well regulated Militia, being necessary to the security of a free State, the right of the people to keep and bear Arms, shall not be infringed."

What does this mean; especially what does "A well regulated Militia," mean since apparently the purpose of the Second Amendment was to establish the right of citizens to arm themselves for the common defense of the country? This was, in fact, what happened in the Revolutionary War, which was fought initially by Militias. This issue came up before the Supreme Court in the 1890's and the court decided essentially that all responsible citizens ("we the people" referred to in the constitution) are part of the Militia regardless of whether they belong to an organized group or not. However, the court also decided that not all citizens are responsible and allowed the government to prevent certain individuals from owning guns. Also, subsequent decisions affirmed the right of the government to control what types of guns citizens could own.

You may legally own a gun or guns and are considered a part of "we the people" and the Militia if:

- You are a US Citizen over the age of 18 (21 for handguns). It is illegal for a non-US Citizen to own a gun in the US.
- You have never been convicted of a felony. (There are exceptions)
- You are not under a domestic violence restraining order.
- You have never been ruled mentally incompetent.
- You are not a drug user (illegal

drugs)

- Other minor rules.

As a result of various laws passed by Congress it is illegal for a citizen to own the following:

- A fully automatic gun (machine gun) unless you have a Class III license (difficult to get, more later)
- A sawed off shotgun or rifle
- A gun with a bore greater than 50 caliber (except shotguns)
- A silencer (Except Class III license)
- Armor piercing bullets
- Certain gadget type guns such as cane guns.

The National Firearms Act of 1934

The first law passed that regulated firearms on a national scale was the National Firearms Act of 1934. This law was the result of the lawlessness and rise of gangster culture during prohibition. President Franklin D. Roosevelt hoped this act would eliminate automatic fire weapons like machine guns from America's streets. Other firearms such as short-barreled shotguns and rifles, parts of guns like silencers, as well as other gadget type firearms hidden in canes and such were also targeted. This law is still in force.

A second part of the law regulated gun sales. All regulated gun sales and gun manufacturers were slapped with a $200 tax (no small amount for Americans mired in the Great Depression; that would be like a tax of $2800 today), and all buyers were required to fill out paperwork subject to Treasury Department Approval. Although parts of this law are still in force subsequent laws have revised it extensively.

The Federal Firearms Act of 1938

In 1938 the Federal Firearms Act was passed. Congress aimed this law at those involved in selling and shipping of firearms through interstate or foreign commerce channels. Anyone involved in the selling of firearms was required to obtain a Federal Firearms License from the Secretary of Commerce ($1 annual fee). They were also required to record the names and addresses of everyone they sold guns to and were prohibited from selling to those people who were convicted of certain crimes or lacked a permit. An amended version of this law is still in force. For instance, there are now several classes of federal firearms licenses all of which have substantial fees and are administered by the Department of Alcohol, Tobacco, and Firearms. Those who have licenses are still required to keep records, and are required to submit information on potential buyers of firearms to ATF for a background check.

The Gun Control Act of 1968

The Gun Control Act of 1968 was passed after the assassination of John F. Kennedy, who allegedly was killed by a mail-order gun that belonged to Lee Harvey Oswald, which inspired this major revision to federal gun laws. The subsequent assassinations of Martin Luther King and Robert Kennedy fueled its quick passage. License requirements were expanded to include more dealers and more detailed record keeping was expected from them. Handgun sales over state lines were restricted. The list of persons dealers could not sell to grew to include those convicted of felonies (with some exceptions), those found mentally incompetent, drug users and more. The act also defined persons who were banned from possessing firearms. This act is largely still in force.

The key element of this bill outlawed mail order sales of rifles and shotguns; Up until this law, mail order consumers only had to sign a statement that they were over 21 years of age for a handgun (18 for rifle or shotgun); it also detailed more persons who were banned from possessing certain guns, including drug users, and further restricted shotgun and rifle sales. These elements of the law are still in force.

Law Enforcement Officers Protection Act and the Firearms Owners Protection Acts of 1986

In 1986 more laws were passed called the Law Enforcement Officers Protection Act and the Firearms Owners Protection Act. These acts made it illegal for anyone to manufacture or import armor piercing ammunition, or "cop-killer bullets," which are capable of penetrating bulletproof clothing. The current controversy concerning green tipped bullets, which are claimed to be capable of penetrating body armor, is based on this law. These acts also eased restrictions on gun sellers and the sale of some guns. Additional penalties were imposed for persons using a firearm during certain crimes and persons with robbery or burglary convictions who are illegally shipping guns.

The Violent Crime Control and Law Enforcement Act of 1994

As a result of a number of school shootings and other postal type shootings the Violent Crime Control and Law Enforcement Act of 1994 was passed. This law expired in 2004 and was not renewed. This law was commonly referred to as the "Assault Weapons Ban," and this bill banned the manufacture, possession, and importation of new semiautomatic assault weapons and large-capacity ammunition feeding devices (or magazines) for civilian use. Criteria for semiautomatic assault weapons that fall under the ban are provided as well as a list of 19 specific firearms. It also prohibits juveniles from possessing or selling handguns and directs the attorney general to evaluate proposed and existing state juvenile gun laws. As will be shown later, the attempt to define assault weapons by appearance rather than by function was perhaps the stupidest law ever passed by Congress, and there are certainly a plethora of laws vying for that title. Nevertheless, there were good features of this law such as limiting magazine capacity, but, unfortunately, there were huge gapping loopholes in this law, which will be discussed later.

The Federal Firearms Licensing System

All gun dealers and manufacturers of guns are required by law to have a license to buy and sell guns. Collectors of firearms may obtain a license that gives them limited rights to buy and sell guns legally. There are nine different classes of licenses. They are:

License Class	Entity holding License
01	Dealer in firearms other than destructive devices, includes Gunsmiths
02	Pawnbroker in firearms other than destructive devices
03	Collector of Curios and Relics
06	Manufacturer of ammunition for firearms
07	Manufacturer of firearms other than destructive devices
08	Importer of firearms other than destructive devices
09	Dealer in destructive devices
10	Manufacturer of destructive devices
11	Importer of destructive devices

Any store or individual that regularly buys and/or sells firearms must have a Class 01 or 02 licenses. All firearms sold by manufacturers and sold interstate must be sold to a Class 01 dealer. One who collects firearms may obtain a Class 03 license which gives him or her the right to buy guns classified as collectable by the ATF through interstate transactions, such as on-line gun auctions and from dealers who ship interstate. All applicants for licenses must send a copy to their local law enforcement

agencies; usually this is the county sheriff and city police. Applicants for certain types of licenses must have the permission of the local law enforcement agencies.

Owners of machine guns and numerous other regulated devices must register them with the ATF. This registration requires the permission of the local law enforcement agencies, and frequently, this permission is denied by such agencies as part of their policies. There is also a substantial fee for this permission, which must be renewed annually.

State Laws

Every state has a number of gun control laws on their books, most dating from the late 19th and early 20th centuries. Texas, for instance, has literally hundreds of such laws. Many of these laws were enacted to give Police the right to charge persons carrying a gun and/or using a gun in a crime with an additional charge.

For instance, the open carry prohibitions were passed to mainly to prevent Blacks and Hispanics from openly carrying a gun, it being presumed that if they were carrying they were up to no good. The law didn't specifically mention race but this was understood. This allowed the Police to stop such people and question them and arrest them if they saw fit to do so. Gradually these laws were applied to White persons as well, however, it was always and still is primarily applied to minorities. There is a movement underway to repeal these laws, however, the proponents of repeal tend to use public relations tactics that tend to backfire. For instance, there have been a number of demonstrations where numbers of these proponents have openly carried rifles and pistols into big box stores. Every parent in the store with children probably wrote their congressperson asking that the laws be kept in force. What if a loaded gun dropped and discharged, killing a child? What if a child grabbed a gun and shot someone? There are dozens of other such scenarios, all ending badly.

The Texas State Rifle Association has a legal column in its magazine, which attempts to clarify state laws concerning guns. The Lawyers writing the articles often find the laws conflicting and confusing. This is typical of many other states as well.

What is a Gun?

Guns have been used since about the 14th century, primarily for warfare, however, it was soon learned they were useful for hunting as well. Guns are a machine, actually a fairly complex machine, whose purpose is to kill, either humans in war or animals while hunting. The machine is designed to propel a projectile, usually made of lead, at high velocity using chemical propellants. The velocity is designed to be high enough to injure or kill any living thing the projectile hits.

I used to have a collection of guns intended to illustrate the evolution of guns starting with a Flintlock Rifle and progressing through cap locks to modern cartridge fed weapons. Today's guns are highly developed machines made of special materials most of which are capable of firing multiple rounds.

Government and Gun Control

As has been seen, the government _does_ have the right to control guns. Some would call this plain old common sense. Guns are dangerous and governments regulate dangerous things. The government dictates who can own a gun, and what types of guns they may own. This is a well-established fact and principle of law. The Supreme Court has upheld both the right of citizens to own guns and the right of government to regulate such ownership.

Chapter 2 – Gun Myths and Facts

The World That Was

I attended High School in the mid-50's. The school had a rifle range under the gym and a rifle club. I was a member and we practiced target shooting once a week before school started. The rifle club received rifles, targets, and ammunition from the Department of Defense Civilian Marksmanship Program. We were given the option of using the club rifles, which were single shot 03 Springfield's in 22 caliber or our own guns. I had a bolt-action single shot 22 rifle that I decided to use. I would take the rifle from home to the bus stop, board the city public transportation bus to go to school carrying this rifle openly in hand, travel to school, changing buses downtown. When I arrived at school we had our practice, then I placed my gun in my locker and locked it with a combination lock. The gun remained there all day. After school I joined my other classmates, openly taking my gun with me, and we boarded the city bus and went home. We had to use city buses and traveled with the public, there were no school buses at that time.

Think of what would happen if a kid tried to board a city bus openly carrying a rifle today. Probably the SWAT team would be called. Today it is illegal for a student to carry a rifle or pistol in school, on a public bus, and much less put it in their locker.

Back then children could walk safely a mile

or more to school and not worry about being kidnapped by a pervert. Home burglaries were rare. Drive by shootings non-existent. School shootings were unheard of. There were drugs but they were deep underground. There were no drug dealers in schools or on street corners. It's not the same world it was then and that must be understood.

How many Guns are there and where are they?

It is estimated that there are 300 million guns; rifles, pistols, and shotguns, in the US, probably a low estimate in a country with 307 million people (from Just Facts.com/gun control). Therefore, theoretically there is nearly one gun per person, however the distribution is skewed. Only 42% of households and 30% of individuals own guns. The poll showed that 70 to 80 million adults owned guns and 40 to 45 million of them owned handguns. Thus approximately one third of the population or slightly less own guns.

Statistics show a few people own a lot of guns each. This is not surprising since guns have specialized uses and a person could easily own a pistol, rifle, and shotgun or several of each, all for different purposes, such as hunting, target shooting and personal defense against crime. In fact, it is quite common for collectors to own many guns, 50 to 100 guns is quite common. At one time my own gun collection held 80 guns, all of which were sold to licensed collectors. Thus almost all guns are owned by only about a third of the population.

In the 19th and early 20th Century's it was common for rural people, and most of the population was rural at that time, to hunt to put meat on the table. However today, there are fewer and fewer hunters and guns are used primarily for target shooting and home defense. In fact, 67% of gun owners said they owned them for home protection. As a result fewer and fewer people own guns.

The fight over gun control

If we look at some foreign countries where the population has become largely urbanized, such as Australia, European nations, Japan, and even Canada, we find that these nations have put increasing restrictions on gun ownership, particularly handguns, but other guns as well. In many of these countries it is illegal to possess a handgun. Ownership of guns is tightly regulated, in most cases the governments require gun owners to be licensed or registered and their guns must also be registered. There are restrictions on how many and what type of guns they may own. Generally, school shootings where numbers of children have been shot and killed has facilitated the passage of these highly restrictive laws, and these laws have proved very effective in eliminating school and mass shootings.

The Wall Street Journal edition of October 5, 2015 reported that between 2000 and 2014 the US reported 166 mass shootings.

This is in contrast to most civilized countries, which rarely reported more than one or two in the same time period. CNN web site on October 6, 2015 quoted FBI sources saying there were 160 incidences of mass shootings between 2000 and 2013, which killed 486 people and wounded 557 people, not counting the shooter or shooters. James Yancone, FBI Assistant Director also said, "In the first half of the years studied, the average number of incidents was 6.4 (per year), but that average rose in the second half of the study to 16.4, an average of more than one incident per month."

Public reaction to school shootings has been surprisingly mild in the US compared to that in the UK, Germany, and Australia. Incidents in those countries generated public initiatives that resulted in political legal action. Perhaps 9-11 has desensitized the American public to mass killings by deranged persons. There will be more mass shootings, which is certain, and the number per year is dramatically increasing. How many will it take for the public to insist on action?

Discover Magazine in its September October 2019 issue had an extensive article on Gun Violence. It reported that in 2017 in the US there were 39,773 deaths due to firearms and 1.625 million deaths since 1968, more than the accumulated deaths of all Americans in all the wars since the countries founding. Astonishing!! There has been a steady rise in deaths by firearms in the US since 2000. Death by firearm now exceed deaths by motor vehicles, yet research spending on death by motor vehicle is 16 times the spending on research on death by firearms. In fact, of the 20 top causes of death, death by firearm is 19th in research funding, being more only that the 20th place which is from falls.

The probability of death by firearm for an individual is five times higher in the US than in other high-income countries. In 2017, handguns were used in 7,032 of the 7,886 homicide deaths where the type of gun used was known. The article recommends public health approach to reducing gun violence, namely requiring gun owners to receive instruction and be licensed similar to auto drivers.

This book was originally written early in 2015 and was revised later that year. This is a complete revision of previous versions because since then more sad statistics have come to light, particularly the increase in frequency and deaths and injuries in mass shootings. The Wall Street Journal reported in the February 17, 2018 issue that three decades of school shootings have resulted in more than 150 deaths of children and adults, and these 70 shootings started in the 90's and the death toll climbs every year. These are just School shootings, many more shootings have occurred such as the Las Vegas shooting and the Sutherland Church El Paso shootings in Texas. The FBI, for instance reported that between 2000 and 2012 there were 160 shootings which injured or killed 1,043 people, and that the rate of shootings was increasing. The Washington Post reported that since 1966 there have been 150 shootings, which have killed four or more people each and killed a total of 1,827 persons. For each killing many more are wounded, often with life long consequences, frequently twice as many are injured as are killed, however, a quick glance at the statistics indicated that slightly more are wounded than are killed.

It can be claimed that the NRA is winning battles and losing the war. The reason is simple, only about one-third of households own guns. We are no longer the rural nation of the early 20th Century; we are the highly urbanized nation of the 21st Century. The two thirds of households that don't own guns can quickly become suspicious of those who do, and this has happened in many countries already. The NRA's extremist stance that no gun law is a good law is simply untenable in the changing political environment. The NRA claims that enforcement of the existing laws would go a long way toward limiting gun ownership by mentally ill and terrorists. This is true, except that the NRA actively campaigns against funding activities on all levels, local, state, and national, that would fund the enforcement of these laws. Particularly they campaign against funding of reporting of felons and those adjudicated as being mentally ill at all levels and have been successful in doing so. Thus the NRA is highly hypocritical when it says existing laws should be enforced and then denies the funding to do so.

The NRA's obsession to support one political party puts all its eggs in one basket, makes it a sub set of that party, and has put it on the outs with Washington several times. The NRA claims 4.5 million members, however the total subscription number for its three magazines is only a little over 3 million, all members get at least one magazine and many members take more than one magazine, and many magazines are sent to libraries, perhaps several thousand, so the actual membership is probably significantly less than 3 million, indeed it may be less than 1.5 million. However, there are approximately 100 million people in homes with guns. Thus the NRA represents only a tiny minority of the gun owning population, about 3% at best, and speaks for an extremist element within that minority.

Recently, the dictatorial reign of Wayne LaPairre, the real head of the NRA, has been challenged. It has been alleged that he has fraudulently diverted NRA funds for personal use and is under investigation by several governmental authorities for fraud and other crimes. The NRA is in danger of imploding.

The reality of Gun Control

Why not make Handguns illegal? Indeed, why not make all guns illegal for the public to own? The following discussion will illustrate why this is not possible.

There are a number of activities humans engage in that are disapproved of by others. Some call some of these activities sin. Attempts have been made to make these activities illegal, all of which have failed. Another strategy is to regulate and tax such activities. Some of these activities are:

- Alcohol consumption, the biggest failure of a law in history was probably prohibition. Alcohol is now regulated and taxed by government.

- Gambling. Gambling has actually been legal throughout most of history. In the 18th and 19th Century's not only was gambling legal, but also gambling debts were recognized as legal debts by the courts and one could actually be jailed for nonpayment. Early in the 20th Century the Prohibitionists also targeted gambling and were successful in making it illegal in most places. Today gambling is still largely illegal but numerous places allow it as a highly regulated activity.

- Prostitution, called the worlds oldest profession. Prostitution is illegal almost everywhere but yet still exists and will continue to exist everywhere.

- Illegal drug use. The war on drugs has been going on since the 20's and hasn't been won yet. There are some drugs that shouldn't have been made illegal such as Marijuana. All drugs have some beneficial uses and making them illegal inhibits such beneficial uses.

- Gun ownership. Gun ownership is regulated by government but is not illegal.

- Sexual Preference. It is now understood that sexual preference is a genetic trait and not a social aberration. It is fast becoming legal for same gender persons to marry and enjoy all the rights of heterosexual couples.

Making activities such as those in the above list illegal merely generates a highly profitable business for criminals. Prohibition was an excellent example of this as is the war on drugs. Prostitution and the human slavery resulting from its illegality are a crime against humanity, yet people insist on not seeing reality. Prostitution has successfully been made legal in some localities with tight government regulation. This has prevented the exploitation of women.

The preferred strategy should be "Regulate and Tax." That's a strategy that will work most of the time. Making anything illegal that people want merely makes a business for criminals and costs the government tax dollars to fight it. The war on drugs is an excellent example of this as was prohibition.

Making guns illegal won't work. Criminals will always be able to obtain any gun they want. Recent attacks by religious extremists in Europe with fully automatic machine guns, which are completely illegal to own, are an example of this. However, government can reduce the availability of guns to terrorists, criminals, and to the mentally ill through regulation and taxation.

Assault weapons

The law later called the Assault Weapons ban attempted to define assault rifles by appearance and not function. It didn't work, primarily because one can only define types of guns by function and not by appearance.

To illustrate this point, in the 50's the Remington Company produced a number of types of hunting rifles called the 700 and later the 7000 series. These guns were intended solely for hunting and target practice and had detachable box magazines that held four rounds. They produced a bolt action, a pump gun, and a semi-automatic in a number of different calibers. For those who don't know, a semi automatic gun will fire one round each time the trigger is pulled. A full automatic will fire rounds as long as the trigger is held down and is known as a machine gun. There were other companies that also produced guns with detachable box magazines including Browning and Winchester. Later, large capacity magazines became available for the Remington's, which were produced by after market suppliers. Thus it was possible to buy high capacity magazines, holding 10 to 30 or more rounds, for these rifles. This made them functionally the equivalent of the rifles banned by the assault weapons ban, but they weren't banned because they didn't have the appearance of an assault weapon. There is no functional difference between a so-called assault weapon and a semi-automatic sporting weapon other than looks.

The real issue is magazine capacity. High capacity magazines are available for nearly all guns, including most sporting rifles, pistols, and shotguns.

There are semi automatic versions of the M-16 and M-4; military rifles that have full automatic capability, sold as civilian guns. The civilian versions, sometimes called AR-15 type rifles, use the same high-capacity magazines as the military versions, but are capable of being fired in semi-automatic mode only, thus are legal to own.

This is a standard semi-automatic Remington 7400 hunting rifle with a standard four round magazine in the stock.

Above is a semi-automatic Bushmaster M-4 with a 30 round magazine. Below is the same Remington with a 10 round high-capacity magazine. Higher capacity magazines have been available for this rifle. Note that the Remington also comes in a carbine version, which would make it the same length as the Bushmaster. Both are semi-automatic and capable of being equipped with high capacity magazines. Both can be equipped with various types of stocks, including collapsible and folding stocks.

The only difference between them is how they look. The Bushmaster would have been classified as an assault weapon under the old Assault Weapons Ban and the Remington would not. The point being made is both weapons are equally capable of mass shootings. Guns should be classified by function and not by appearance.

From a function standpoint, there is no difference between AR-15 type guns and a semi-automatic Remington 700 or 7000 series hunting rifle equipped with a high-capacity magazine.

Chapter 3 – Crime and Guns

Handguns, the elephant in the room

One doesn't see drug dealers standing on corners selling their wares with AK-47's, or civilian versions of M-16's or M-4's strapped to their backs. No, that would be a bit obvious, however, it is highly likely they have a small handgun hidden somewhere on their person. They are in a dangerous business, actually most of the danger is from other drug dealers and competing gangs and they need protection.

Most criminals prefer handguns for obvious reasons. They are concealable but can be produced quickly during the perpetration of a crime and reconcealed afterwards.

Handguns are very intimidating and usually result in the victim doing what the criminal wants.

Most crimes involving firearms utilize handguns. In 1993, 582,000 reported murders, robberies, and aggravated assaults were committed with firearms. Murder was the crime that most frequently involved the discharge of firearms; 70% of the 24,526 murders in 1993 were committed with firearms. (From US Bureau of Justice statistics).

There is a movement to ban handguns. It won't work for the same reasons making guns illegal won't work. Handguns, especially the small handguns favored by criminals and those who have concealed weapons permits, interestingly, usually have small magazines or cartridge capacities. This makes them small and concealable, and in fact, studies show that in a confrontational situation one rarely gets off more than three shots. A large capacity magazine or high capacity is simply not needed for personal protection or for criminal activity. Most 380 semi-automatic pistols, the ones favored for conceal ability, have 6 round magazines, and most small revolvers hold only five or four shots. A successful criminal, defining success as taking a lot of money in a robbery or other illegal action, will never have to fire his weapon and therefore, has no need for a high capacity magazine.

It is not going to be possible to remove all handguns, or any other gun currently legal, by making them illegal. As the slogan goes, "If guns are outlawed, only outlaws will have guns." Actually, the same thing that happened during Prohibition will happen; common citizens will become the outlaws. The slogan should read, "If guns are outlawed, citizens will become outlaws." There is, however, a way to reduce the number and to insure those who own them are responsible.

High Capacity Magazines

Generally, school shooters and mass murderers prefer semi-automatic rifles, usually the AR-15 type. The reason is simple; rifles with high capacity magazines allow more people to be shot in a shorter length of time. Further, Rifles have a longer range, better accuracy, and people can be shot at greater distances than with a pistol.

There are pistols with high capacity magazines, but the large number of rounds requires that the pistol be made larger to accommodate the size of the magazine. Military pistols and the pistols used by police generally have high capacity magazines, 15 rounds for a 9 mm as used in the standard M9 military version of the Beretta being a common number. It is possible to obtain 20, 30, and 40 round magazines for such pistols, but the magazine will stick out several inches from the bottom of the hand grip, making the pistol difficult to holster and difficult to handle.

The assault weapons ban also prohibited the

manufacture of magazines with more than 10 rounds after 1994; however, it did not ban the importation of high capacity magazines that had been manufactured before 1994. There were a plethora of high capacity magazines for various guns sold at gun shows and on the Internet that claimed to have been manufactured before that date. Most were from China but there were others from other countries. On inspection, it was obvious these were of new manufacture; the producer had merely certified they were made before 1994. Thus there was a huge loophole in the law through which literally container loads of high capacity magazines were driven.

When it comes to criminal acts, high capacity magazines benefit mass murderers, and these are people who are mentally ill. The common criminal has no need of such a magazine, the possible exception being gang members who need them to defend against rival gangs.

Limiting the capacity of magazines to 10 rounds would mean that mass murderers would need to switch magazines more frequently, an act taking a short amount of time. This would give police an instant to use to neutralize the threat.

There is no sporting reason to have a gun with a magazine with a capacity of more than 10 rounds. More on this later.

Mental Health and Guns

Those who have been convicted of a felony (there are exceptions), are under a domestic violence restraining order, or have been ruled mentally incompetent are not permitted to own guns. Actually, thanks to a lack of funding, the records for such people are often not transmitted to the ATF, so such people can often buy guns and pass the ATF background check. The Sutherland Church shooter had a domestic violence restraining order and should not have been able to buy the gun he used, but the order had never been reported to the ATF as required by law. The record keeping and transmittal system needs to be updated so the ATF information is current. Funding needs to be provided at all levels of government to support this effort.

There is another class of felons who are extremely dangerous. These are people who have anger management problems, are prone to violence, and have guns. There has been a number of road rage shooting incidents recently, some of which have resulted in the death of the victim. All these are, by definition, perpetrated by people with anger management problems who have guns.

The following article illustrates this point:

Nearly 1 in 10 Adults Has Impulsive Anger Issues and Access To Guns

By Duke Medicine News and Communications

DURHAM, N.C. – An estimated 9 percent of adults in the U.S. have a history of impulsive, angry behavior and have access to guns, according to a study published this month in Behavioral Sciences and the Law. The study also found that an estimated 1.5 percent of adults report impulsive anger and carry firearms outside their homes.

Angry people with ready access to guns are typically young or middle-aged men, who at times lose their temper, smash and break things, or get into physical fights, according to the study co-authored by scientists at Duke, Harvard, and Columbia universities.

Study participants who owned six or more firearms were also far more likely than people with only one or two firearms to carry guns outside the home and to have a history of impulsive, angry behavior.

"As we try to balance constitutional rights and public safety regarding people with mental illness, the traditional legal approach has been to prohibit firearms from involuntarily-committed psychiatric patients," said Jeffrey Swanson, Ph.D., professor in psychiatry and behavioral sciences at Duke Medicine and lead author of the study. "But now we have more evidence that current laws don't necessarily keep firearms out of the hands of a lot of potentially dangerous individuals."

The researchers analyzed data from 5,563 face-to-face interviews conducted in the National Comorbidity Study Replication (NCS-R), a nationally representative survey of mental disorders in the U.S. led by Harvard in the early 2000s.

The study found little overlap between participants with serious mental illnesses and those with a history of impulsive, angry behavior and access to guns.

"Gun violence and serious mental illness are two very important but distinct public health issues that intersect only at their edges," Swanson said.

Researchers found that anger-prone people with guns were at elevated risk for a range of fairly common psychiatric conditions such as personality disorders, alcohol abuse, anxiety, and post-traumatic stress, while only a tiny fraction suffered from acute symptoms of major disorders such as schizophrenia and bipolar disorder.

Fewer than one in 10 angry people with access to guns had ever been admitted to a hospital for a psychiatric or substance abuse problem, the study found. As a result, most of these individuals' medical histories wouldn't stop them from being able to legally purchase guns under existing mental-health-related restrictions.

"Very few people in this concerning group suffer from the kinds of disorders that often lead to involuntary commitment and which would legally prohibit them from buying a gun," said Ronald Kessler, Ph.D., professor of health care policy at Harvard and principal investigator of the NCS-R survey.

Kessler, Swanson and co-authors reason that looking at a prospective gun buyer's history of misdemeanor convictions, including violent offenses and multiple convictions for impaired driving, could be more effective at preventing gun violence in the U.S. than screening based on mental health treatment history.

As for those who already own or have access to firearms, the researchers suggest the data could support "dangerous persons" gun removal laws, like those in Connecticut and Indiana, or a "gun violence restraining order" law like California recently enacted. Such laws give family members and law enforcement a legal tool to immediately seize guns and prevent gun or ammunition purchases by people who show warning signs of impending violence.

In 2012, more than 59,000 people were injured by the intentional use of firearms, and another 11,622 were killed in violent gun incidents, according to the Centers for Disease Control and Prevention.

The Duke, Harvard, and Columbia analysis appears in a special issue of the journal Behavioral Sciences and the Law that focuses on mental illness and gun violence. The article presents the first national estimates of the number of people who have access to guns and who also have a history of angry, impulsive behavior, with or without a diagnosable mental illness.

In addition to Swanson and Kessler, study authors include Nancy A. Sampson, Maria V. Petukhova, and Alan M. Zaslavsky of Harvard, Paul S. Appelbaum of Columbia, and Marvin S. Swartz of Duke.

The original survey used in the study, the NCS-R, is supported by the National Institute of Mental Health (U01-MH60220) with supplemental support from the National Institute on Drug Abuse, the Substance Abuse and Mental Health Services Administration, the Robert Wood Johnson Foundation (044780), the

John W. Alden Trust, and the Elizabeth K. Dollard Trust.

###

The study went on to recommend that people convicted of misdemeanors for violent crimes should be excluded from buying guns.

Chapter 4 _Lessons from Massacres

Recent massacres can teach us some lessons.

The Las Vegas Massacre

The shooter in Las Vegas shot from a high point in a hotel, shooting down on a rock concert. He shot multiple semiautomatic rifles equipped with "bump stocks" which enabled them to be fired at a rate similar to machine guns, thus greatly increasing the death toll. The death toll would have been much higher except the shooter was involved in a shooting altercation with the hotel security guard and the SWAT team was already on its way and knew where the shooter was. Thus they were able to respond unusually quickly and shot the shooter. Even so

58 people lost their lives and a large number were wounded.

The main lesson from this incident is manufacturers of after market parts have found ways to make semi-automatic weapons into machine guns. These include not only the "Bump Stock" but also the "Trigger Bouncer and other devices. These devices should be banned, and made illegal to own. They could also be put on the list of dangerous devices, like machine guns, and require permission and permits to own. Recently bump stocks were banned, however, other devices are still available legally.

Silencers. Also a prohibited device, are also making their way into to the hands of gun owners through a legal loophole which lawyers created. This loophole needs to be plugged.

The Sutherland Texas Church Shooting

In this incident a man entered a church and shot 26 people with an AR-15 rifle with a high capacity magazine. He was confronted by police and shot.

This man had been convicted of domestic abuse charges while in the service but the Department of Defense had not reported this to the BATF so he was not on the list of people who were prohibited from owning a gun. He bought the gun legally illustrating the point that many government agencies, including the Department of Defense, are not reporting people to the BATF and the BATF list is not complete. Many government agencies at all levels have failed to report, local, county, state, and federal. It requires time and effort to report and the excuse given is they don't have the funds to make the effort. This has been going on for literally decades and there are possibly millions of people who should be on the list but aren't. All can legally buy firearms. This needs to be corrected.

The Parkland High School Shooting

In this case a mentally ill 19 year old obtained several guns and used an AR-15 rifle to kill 17 people and injure 12 others.

The FBI actually received a report that this person was planning the shooting and did nothing. The FBI needs to look at its procedures and change them so it can react to information such as this.

The El Paso Wall Mart Shooting

In this case a young man drove from Dallas to El Paso with the specific intent to kill Hispanics.

His mother had called the police a week earlier warning them that her son was potentially dangerous. The Police ignored the warning. He killed 22 people and wounded another 8. Police need to take all threats seriously and there need to be laws making such threats illegal, in fact, there are such laws in a number of states.

Chapter 5 - Solutions that will not work and why.

Should Teachers be Armed?

It has been suggested by a number of people that teachers be armed. This comes under the heading of "What can possibly go wrong?" The answer is just about everything.

The first problem is where would a teacher keep their weapon? Children are naturally inquisitive and into all sorts of things, no teacher can keep track of 20 to 30 kids all the time, so the gun would have to be securely locked somewhere the kids would not be able to get it, but it would also make it hard for the teacher to obtain it.

My wife has taught in many different schools. There are two main methods to keep teacher's private belongings safe, lockers in the teacher's lounge and a lockable drawer in their classroom desk. Keeping a gun in the locker is impractical for obvious reasons; it would be to far away for the teacher to get it when the shooting starts. Keeping in in a locked drawer is also dangerous, my wife has had kids break into locked drawers and steal money from her purse. What if there was a gun there? The results of that are scenario are easily imagined, death or injury of one or more students is the likely result.

Confronting a shooter requires extensive training, so teacher would have to be trained. I have taken such training from an Israeli expert and it is rigorous and requires a lot of time. The cost to school district would be thousands of dollars for each teacher for weapons storage devices and training. It is simply not practical. Teachers and students would be far better off if the teacher used the limited time to herd the students to safety or if necessary, to barricade the room and keep the students calm.

There are a number of problems in confronting an active shooter. First is the defender is likely to be mistaken for the shooter by the arriving police or security guards. When they see a person with a gun and hear gunshots, they will immediately conclude anyone with a gun who is not in uniform is an active shooter and react accordingly. The other problem is, unless one has received extensive training and is a good shot; the probability of hitting an innocent bystander is very great.

It's best to leave confrontations to armed security guards or police, the exception being if one has received special training and can react quickly enough before the police get there. My instructor could draw his concealed pistol and fire four or more shots accurately into a target representing an active shooter in almost a blink of an eye, but he had trained for years to do that with the Israeli armed forces and Israeli anti-terrorist police squads.

If schools are very concerned they should hire armed guards and install security devices such as electronic locks to lockdown the building, and well as cameras and monitors to spot a shooter, and that is just the beginning of possible security measures.   In fact a mass shooting was prevented in California because an observant desk clerk locked the building down.

In such a situation experts advise running, and if that is not possible, hiding, and if that is not possible, attack the shooter because your chances are not very good at that point.

Government Inaction Is Not Working

Our government has taken virtually no action in the last three decades to prevent mass shootings. Hillary Clinton opposed the NRA in the last election and gained three million more votes than her opponent, proving the NRA is not a voter powerhouse. Politicians need to realize that opposing the NRA will not loose them the election and they need to develop a backbone and get to work doing their job of protecting our children and us.

The Israelis have been fighting terrorism for over a century and have effective means to limit attacks. The US Government needs to study what the Israelis have done and apply their lessons to our situation.

Concealed Handgun Licensees should be able to stop an active shooter.

It was suggested by a gun advocate that if CHL holders were present at the Wal-Mart in El Paso then the shooter would have been stopped. First, there were undoubtedly some CHL holders in the store; there were several hundred people in the store and in the parking lot, so why didn't any of them stop him?   The percentage of people who hold CHL's is quite high in Texas so there had to be a number of them at the shooting.

So let's imagine Joe CHL is in the store and hears gunshots. First he has to determine where the shots are coming from and go toward them. Not something most people would do, most will be running away from the gunshots.   But suppose he runs toward the shots and sees the shooter. There are people running everywhere so does he draw his gun and shoot at the shooter?   Suppose the shooter moves or he misses, he is likely to hit an innocent bystander. Remember it is chaotic scene and everyone is moving, including the shooter, so the probability he will hit the shooter is actually quite small. Further many shooters have bulletproof vests and other defensive equipment.

The next problem he faces is when the police arrive, and they usually arrive quite quickly, he's holding a gun dressed in civilian clothes, how are the police going to know he is not the shooter. They aren't, and are as likely to shoot him as the real shooter.

Limit the Fire Rate of Semi-Automatics

As manufactured most semi-automatic weapons, both pistols and rifles, can fire a round with each pull of the trigger. A typical AR-15 type rifle is reported to have a rate of fire of 45 rounds per minute, however, I can fire at least two rounds per second so that number must be based on the fact the shooter will have to change the magazine. Most magazines hold 30 rounds so a rate of fire of 45 rounds per minute would allow about 38.5 seconds to change the magazine, which is probably about right. It is possible to attain a fairly high rate of fire merely by pulling the trigger quickly repeatedly. Revolvers and pump and bolt action weapons require much more effort and time to fire and cannot be fired at as high a rate as a semi-automatic.

Manufacturers can limit the fire rate of semi-automatics by design, in fact, at least one semi-auto pistol, the Browning BDM, was designed with a lever which allowed it to be operated either in semi-automatic mode or in double action revolver mode. Most semi-autos cock the hammer and reset the firing pin when a new shell is loaded, thus only requiring one to pull the trigger to release the firing pin. That allows for rapid fire. A double action revolver cocks the hammer with trigger action before it can fire, i. e., when one pulls the trigger at first the hammer cocks then releases to hit the firing pin. This requires a longer time between trigger pulls to fire. Not only could this feature be built into all semi-autos, pistols and rifles, but also it would slow down the rate of fire by probably half. If semi-automatic weapons are not to be banned entirely, and they should be, it should be made a requirement that all new and all existing semiautomatics be modified to have this feature. Unfortunately, such a feature is probably easily bypassed or removed by people with mechanical skills so it should be considered an interim measure at best.

Chapter 6 - Common Sense Recommendations for Gun Control

Guns are machines designed specifically to kill. Anyone with a machine shop can make any kind of gun. John Browning made prototypes of working guns from raw metal in a small shop that was 10 by 20 feet with only a lathe, milling machine, and a drill press. He had numerous hand tools as well. In that small space he made everything from semi-automatic pistols to the Browning machine gun. Not only can any machinist make a gun, but also some are claiming 3D printers can also make guns.

Why is it we require automobile drivers to obtain licenses and not gun owners?

Automobiles are designed as transportation devices but if operated by a driver that is either not able to control the vehicle, or makes a mistake, or is incapacitated for some reason, can kill in an accident. To make sure all drivers understand the rules and laws governing the operation of a motor vehicle, we require everyone who drives to pass a test ascertaining whether they have the requisite skill and knowledge to be a driver. They are required to buy a license to drive, and are required to renew it periodically.

In fact, all dangerous items such as explosives, hazardous chemicals and materials, and a host of other things are highly regulated. Extensive training is required for the people that handle such items and they are required to have a license. Also permits are required for operations using such items. Why aren't guns regulated like this? They are certainly dangerous.

Anyone with a clean record and who meets the other background check requirements can buy a gun, whether they know how to operate it or not and whether they are aware of the laws concerning gun use or not. They are not required to know anything about gun safety. A person was actually observed buying a simple gun in a gun store and the seller had to show the buyer how to load the gun and how to operate it. The gun was probably more dangerous to the buyer in this case than to anyone else, but the lack of knowledge of the purchaser certainly presented a danger to not only themselves but to everyone else in range of the gun.

Some years ago most states started to require hunters take a hunter safety course before they could buy a hunting license. Hunting deaths and injuries, which were always the result of one hunter shooting another or themselves by accident, declined sharply.

Most states have concealed weapons permits or licenses, which allow persons to carry concealed weapons. In most cases, to obtain such a license one must take a course in gun laws and pass a marksmanship test. In Texas this was an 8-hour course and covered all aspects of gun ownership, especially when one could and when one could not use deadly force.

So, why is it anyone who can pass a background check can buy a gun, regardless of how little they know about gun operation, safety, and gun laws? Shouldn't they first be vetted with such knowledge? Why not require all gun owners and wannabe owners take a course and obtain a license before they can buy or own a gun?

It has recently been revealed that people are buying multiple guns in the US and transporting them to Mexico to sell to the drug gangs. While this is illegal, it is only a misdemeanor. This should be a felony carrying a significant amount of mandatory prison time.

Here is a proposed list of Gun Controls that should be implemented. Contrary to what is sure to be claimed, none of these will trample on anyone's Second Amendment Rights.

- Ban the importation, manufacture, and sale of high capacity magazines or guns capable of holding more than 10 rounds.
- Require background checks for <u>all</u> gun sales. Currently only gun sales by licensed dealers are required to fill out the ATF forms and the purchaser is required to pass a background check. There are a significant number of guns traded by individuals where no background check is

required. This is the primary source of guns for criminals and a means by which terrorists and the mentally ill can obtain guns.

* Ban the importation of all guns and gun parts. This proved to be the big loophole in the Assault weapons ban. Further, imported kits with all parts except the receiver are available with which a competent person can construct a machine gun. Many guns that have been imported are of low quality and some are actually dangerous to use. This ban would please US gun manufacturers but might cause problems with the World Trade Organization, however, many nations ban the importation of firearms.

- Initiate a buy back program for high capacity magazines. Eventually make it illegal to own such magazines.

- Require all gun owners to take gun safety classes similar to the Concealed Handgun classes, and renew them every five years. (Hunters are required to do this now.) Automobile drivers are required to be licensed, why not people who plan to own guns. A gun is at least as dangerous as an Automobile, perhaps more so. Obtaining the license would not necessarily mean the licensee owns a gun or guns, not everyone who has a drivers license owns a car.

- Consider taxing gun and bullet sales, proceeds would go to crime victim's funds.

- Increase jail time for crimes committed with firearms.

- Add persons with misdemeanor convictions for violent crimes to the ban list for purchasing guns.

- Make straw purchasing a felony with mandatory jail time.

- Update the ATF records system so all records of people who are banned from owning a gun are in the system. This will require some states and localities to properly fund and update their systems. There are huge omissions in the BATF list, in fact, probably up to one million or more people should be on that list but aren't because the authorities have not reported to the BATF. Recently, after the Texas Church massacre, it was found that the Department of Defense had not been reporting for decades.

- Pass a Federal Law similar to "dangerous persons" gun removal laws, like those in Connecticut and Indiana, or a "gun violence restraining order" law like California recently enacted. Such laws give family members and law enforcement a legal tool to immediately seize guns and prevent gun or ammunition purchases by people who show warning signs of impending violence.

- Ban the sale of gun kits, which allow a person to manufacture their own gun without any controls or reporting. Such kits are sold with all the parts to make a gun except the receiver is incomplete.

The buyer can, with minimal skills, complete the receiver and assemble a complete gun. No license is required to do this and kit sales are not regulated, so criminals or anyone else can make their own gun.

- Ban the sale of, and make illegal, any device that enables a semi-automatic firearm to be fired rapidly similar to a machine gun. The Las Vegas massacre death toll was high because the perpetrator was equipped with such devices.

- Require all semi-automatic pistols and rifles to be designed to operate like a double action pistol, thus slowing down the rate of fire.

All of the above are doable. The shrillest opposition will come from the NRA, but it represents less than 3% of gun owners and less than 1% of the population. There are many moderates within the NRA including the Author, so the NRA doesn't even represent the opinions of all its members. The NRA leadership is a toothless; blind, crippled troll ranting intensely partisan political mantras and howling shrilly about supposed lack of freedom under the bridge of anachronism. It is so intensely supportive of one political party that that party is quite happy to send speakers to tell the organization what they want to hear. However, this party knows the NRA is in its pocket and will ignore it if public opinion is opposite what the NRA's position is. The problem with a lobbying organization that is tied to one political party is it will be taken for granted and ignored. Worse yet, when politics change, it will be completely ineffective.

There are undoubtedly many groups that will support these changes. Foremost among these groups will be law enforcement organizations. No officer wants to shoot a suspect, yet it is occurring with increasing frequency as persons with anger management problems confront officers. Further, police organizations have long campaigned against open carry. Non-uniformed persons openly carrying weapons present a threat to all of the public. We don't live in the Wild West anymore. Note that undercover officers always carry concealed weapons. Any program that reduces the chance an officer will have to shoot and possibly kill a suspect will be welcomed and supported by law enforcement organizations.

The original idea behind the Second Amendment is that responsible armed citizens would be available for national defense as part of a Militia. The Militia gave such citizens training in the military use of firearms. In the 18th Century nearly everyone had a firearm both for protection and for hunting and was taught from a very young age the safe and proper use and care of guns. Hunting was a major activity that supplied meat for the table. Gradually the Militias disappeared and eventually the Supreme Court decided that everyone who could belong to a Militia ("we the people") should have the right to own a firearm. However, it also allowed the government to restrict certain types of guns and ammunition for the public good.

Today, most people do not own a gun, nor are they knowledgeable in the laws concerning the use of firearms. I remember seeing a woman in a Concealed Weapons Class being taught how to load a gun. She had never handled a firearm before and to her credit, obtained training via the class. The instructors very patiently showed her how to load, cock, and fire the gun, initially using plastic dummy bullets.

It is not in the public interest to allow anyone to own a gun; especially those who have no idea how to use it, have no training in gun safety, and do not know what laws govern their use. It is time for organizations representing gun interests to advocate responsible requirements for gun ownership to include training in both the use of firearms, safety, and the laws governing their use. It is also time for organizations claiming to represent gun owners to insist on proper funding of existing gun laws, especially the reporting requirements.

The End

Glossary

Not in alphabetical order

Gun: A machine or device that utilizes a enclosed chamber (barrel) and ignites a chemical propellant to fire a projectile through that barrel toward an target with a high enough velocity with the intent of striking a living object with enough force to injure or kill. Note that compressed air or gas is also used as a propellant in some guns.

Semi-Automatic Gun: A gun that fires one round each time the trigger is depressed.

Automatic Gun, aka, Machine Gun: A gun that fires rounds continuously as long as the trigger is depressed. Firing ends either when the trigger is released or the gun runs out of ammunition.   Also called full automatic to differentiate it from pistols that are sometimes misnamed automatics.

Magazine: A box made of metal or plastic with a spring in the bottom and open top designed to feed cartridges to the gun. Cartridges are placed in the box and it is inserted into the box holder in the gun. The spring will help feed the cartridges into the receiver as they are fired.

Cartridge or Shell: A round metal or plastic cylindrical container designed to hold chemical propellants. One end is closed and has a primer, and the other end is open but has a projectile (bullet) pressed into it.

When a cartridge is inserted into a gun barrel and the primer is struck by the firing pin, the chemical propellant is ignited and forces the projectile out of the barrel at high velocity.

Chemical Propellant: a chemical, usually powder, that when ignited burns very quickly generating a large amount of gas. Propellants used in modern guns are various formulations of nitrocellulose which is much more powerful than the black powder used in antique guns. Firing a modern nitrocellulose cartridge in a black powder firearm will result in the gun exploding and harming the shooter.

Pistol: A gun with a short barrel and a handgrip. <u>Semi-automatic pistols</u> are commonly called Automatics but are not capable of full automatic fire. <u>Revolvers</u> have a cylinder behind the barrel to hold the cartridges. Single shot, bolt action, and double-barreled pistols are also made. A *single action* revolver is operated by manually cocking the hammer, which also rotates the cylinder, then pulling the trigger which releases the hammer to strike the firing pin which fires the gun. A *double action* revolver cocks the hammer and rotates the cylinder as the trigger is pulled then as the trigger continues to be pulled it releases the hammer, striking the firing pin and firing the gun.

Rifle: A gun with a stock intended to be placed against the shooters shoulder for firing and generally with a longer barrel than a pistol.

Shotgun: A type of rifle that shoots shot shells, i. e., multiple projectiles in the same shell. They are generally used to hunt birds, for sporting shoots, and for home defense.

Round: One cartridge or shot or shell

Caliber: the diameter of the projectile

Black Powder: An antique type of chemical propellant made of Saltpeter, Sulfur, and Charcoal. It is used primarily in muzzle loading guns, however, black powder cartridges were and are made for antique guns.

Cap Lock: A muzzle-loading gun that uses

a cap to ignite black powder. Cap locks were the most common type of gun used during the Civil War.

Flint Lock: A type of gun that used the striking action of flint on steel to ignite a small amount of black powder in a pan, which then ignited the main charge in the barrel. Muzzle loading flintlock guns were used in the Revolutionary War and the War of 1812.

Author's Information

Ralph L. Stephenson, BS, MS, PE, is a professional environmentalist who retired from his position as the Environmental Manager of a multi-billion dollar engineering and construction company with worldwide operations and projects. He has traveled extensively and managed environmental issues for projects in dozens of countries. He is an internationally recognized expert in environmental science and technology, and is presently writing science fiction novels with the theme of climate change. These visionary novels give scientifically based projections of the effects of climate change and the configuration of the coming post-climate change world.

This is his fifth non-fiction work. Two are a graduate level engineering textbook and a book about the Bible, money and economics. All books are available on Amazon.com. The six science fiction novels and one historical novel currently available are:

1. The Confederation Galactica
2. Toy Boy and the Astrologer
3. The Second Expedition
4. The Tentacles of Time
5. Nothing is What it Seems,
6. The Lion of Lade, a Viking Novel
7. A Matter of Survival

Non-Fiction works of general interest currently available are:

1. My Family – Plunkett, Clore, Steele, and Stephenson. A history of my family, homesteading, and Kansas.

2. Publish Free!!!. How to publish your work on Amazon's Createspace and Kindle.

3. Biblical Living. A book about what the Bible says about how to live our lives.

4. Home Bartending Made Simple. How to stock a home bar and make mixed drinks.

5. Common Sense Gun Control. This book,

6. Common Sense Doomsday Prepping. How to prepare for the Apocalypse.

7. The Seven Religions of the Bible.

An exegesis of the seven religions of the Bible.

8. Job, the 21st Century Version.   A modern retelling of the ancient story of Job of the Bible.

9. Ralph's Rough Rules for Success.

10. The Seven Temples of God.